BRING HOME
THE SCORE

A Private Tutor's Guide to Scoring in the Highest Echelons of the SAT, ACT, SHSAT, GRE, GMAT, LSAT, NCLEX, MCAT, or any other Standardized Test

W. Walter Tinsley

For my daughter. I am sometimes not sure that you know just how much warmth and light you've spread in this world.

The Scary Legal Stuff:

I always wondered if there's a potential lawsuit waiting to be filed against all the people that make all sorts of outrageous claims to copyright on what is obviously public domain, fair use, or material that is outside the protection of copyright law. In fact, there's at least one mainstream publisher that makes its money exclusively by asserting worthless legal claims (like the above) onto public domain works before selling them. How is that legal or ethical? Do you remember the time that a certain soft drink company tried to claim copyright to Santa Claus? Seriously. Because it's so hard to say "good corporate stewardship" without trying to appropriate broad sections of the commonweal. So, I would go on to write you about the level of legal gravity I place into little paragraphs asserted in the prefatory components of books, and which parts of this book are legal to freely copy or derive your own material from, but then I could be held liable for practicing law without a license. So I won't do that. Does anyone else see how the current arrangement of things is a mess? Does anyone else see how the current arrangement is a curtailment of the incalculable public goods that are public domain and clear copyright protection? Something to think about.

CONTENTS

ACKNOWLEDGMENTS

With special thanks to the network of family, friends, students, clients, and coaches that helped me build this. This is more your story than mine.

1) The Ahistorical Opportunity and The Importance of Standardized Tests

In simple terms, luck is the intersection of preparation and opportunity.
— Lucius Seneca

Before the wide adoption of standardized tests in this country, it was rare for anyone outside the circle of wealth or connections of a few ethnicities to progress into the upper echelons of society. Even the man who would become the most powerful American of the twentieth century was relegated to the secondary newspaper at Yale because of his "antecedents."

The doors are now possibly more open than they've ever been. Bribery and intimidation by the powerful are now too expensive and treacherous a path for most. (The author has witnessed attempts at both come to naught.) Even then, most colleges now expect you to perform actual coursework for your grades. The beauty of these tests is that they can showcase your intelligence and capacity in a more or less fair and neutral environment. Some will say that the tests are biased. There is some truth to this. Jean Piaget threw out the first two intelligence tests because the girls kept outscoring the boys. Others will say that grades and test scores do not show the whole picture. They are correct. All the tests show are your foreground to the material and your ability to perform difficult cognitive tasks within a time constraint.

The British Empire governed the globe for three and a half

centuries from a talent pool of a wide aristocracy. Our talent pool is immeasurably greater. How much grander could our own initiatives be if we kept good education accessible, our society open, and the tests fair?

See if you can take a good look in the mirror and just decide, come what may, to do your best.

And who knows what we might build?

My Goal in Writing This Book

It's not a big secret that the wealthy have tremendous advantages over the rest of the population. My goal with this text has been to level the playing field as much as possible. Private tutors like myself can be expensive, and even group classes can become a substantial investment. I like to think that a motivated student can extract from this system everything a group class or private tutor has to offer (or more) at a fraction of the cost. Stand on your own two feet. You might like the view. :)

The Cultural Meaning of Standardized Tests

Much of the modern world has adopted standardized testing as its de facto maturity ritual. Parents have a certain role to play in preparing you for the test but cannot help you in the testing arena. Regardless of the outcome, your parents are expected to welcome you back after the test. That said, you will nonetheless be on your own during the trial.

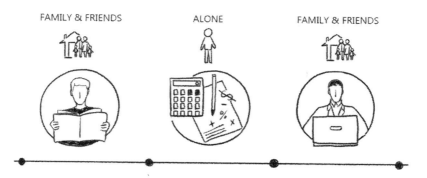

However, instead of assessing your physical prowess, the tests are designed to assess how clever, perceptive, and logical you can be. And the tests are mostly fair, especially at the upper levels. Energy in, energy out; there is essentially nothing else you can do to benefit your future more than bring home a high standardized test score.

I might also note that standardized test scores have a surprising way of coloring your life. Teachers in Florida in 2015 found that their SAT and ACT test scores from all those years and decades before were now being tied to a bonus system to attract and keep higher quality educators.

One of my students told me that her older brother, a young man who had recently been recruited into a New York City investment bank, was asked for his SAT score not only during the application process, but also in the "office talk" his ambitious coworkers tossed around to rank and grade themselves.

The reality of our modern economy is that you can and will be judged for the value you bring to the market and the world. While perhaps harsh, this is an immeasurably better system than the default state of nature of agrarian and industrial economies, namely a class or caste system. It might be pleasant to be born into an upper caste of a certain country, but over a period of time it is inevitable that you and your people will be assimilated or conquered by a society that more efficiently processes its talent pool.

Enough people hold enough positions of power from legacy contacts as it is. Interestingly, these same people are the ones most invested in obstructing your way. Something to think about.

Dilemma of a College Admissions Officer

In abstract terms, the college admissions process is designed to identify who is the most academically qualified and likely to succeed in college in as unbiased terms as possible. Some colleges have other criteria besides academic strengths, and some colleges are more selective than others, but that is the process in its outline.

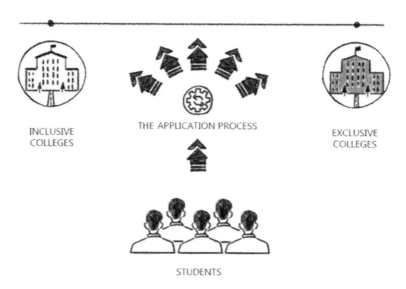

INCLUSIVE
COLLEGES

THE APPLICATION PROCESS

EXCLUSIVE
COLLEGES

STUDENTS

I'm going to argue that this is more or less a fair process in that the standards involved are about your math, critical reading (and, by implication, critical thinking), and writing skills, and not about, say, what ethnic category you belong to, what side of the war your grandparents were on, what religion you or your mother do or do not hold in your hearts, whether you father belonged to the "correct" political party, whether you've inherited a frail bone structure, how much money you or your parents make, or similar topics.

A student might ask, "Can't they get the information they need from my school record and GPA?" This is a reasonable question. I'd like to give the response from the point of view of a college admissions officer. Your GPA is at least in part a reflection of your merits, to be sure, but it is also distorted by a number of factors. As Malcolm Gladwell underscores in his excellent book about the interplay between luck and initiative, *Outliers*, having good teachers, even in bad schools, can have more of an impact on your education than adequate teachers in good schools. All those topics mentioned earlier, in addition to race, gender, class, political and/or religious affiliations, your local real estate tax base, the educational legacies of your state or county, and plain old-fashioned luck, all have a much larger effect on your GPA.

There's also a second, often neglected, component to this discussion. Namely, grade inflation. In scholarly terms, grade inflation is giving a student a higher grade for less effort or an effort that would have received a lower grade in the past. As a tutor, I see this as the intersection of where unmotivated students meet unmotivated teachers. A 3.8 at one school can indicate that I'm likely to be working with a student who can breeze through all my introductory flashcards in twenty or so minutes. A 3.8 at another school might indicate that a student doesn't know how to add fractions, hasn't read a book since elementary school, and has never read a newspaper or magazine article in its entirety in her life. A 3.8 at that same school could also indicate a bright young student who learns quickly, reads 10 or so books a year, but hasn't felt the need to turn in a single homework assignment since her second semester as a freshman.

As a student, I'm sure you've also met people who may be bright enough, but either never do the assigned lessons or give up and stop as soon as the material gets hard. Your college presumably would rather not have this student's name in its rolls. And since GPA is such an unreliable indicator, they typically want a second data point, specifically a test that reveals how well a student performs in an academic environment. Enter standardized testing.

In abstract terms, your college wants to know, should one of your professors assign a chapter in a book or an article to read, whether you will be able to pick out or summarize the main point of the article. Perhaps there is a part of the article where the author offers an aside. Would you be able to follow that tangent and see how it contributes (or takes away) from the main point of the article? If the author uses a specialized term to describe a rare or technical issue, do you know that term, or can you infer what that word means?

"Do you, like, know how to read?" - Your college admissions officer

There's a further component to standardized testing that I don't see mentioned in much of the literature, namely that in order to score in the upper echelons, you will have to have mastered or exposed yourself to a number of abstract and dry concepts. This is a skill unto itself, and a very valuable one. As your college admissions officer can only infer as to whether or not your classes were rigorous, a high standardized test score can unequivocally demonstrate that you have the capacity to become fluent with difficult and abstract material.

If you're reading this, I assume that you have at least an aspiration to be successful in life. Do you really want to go to college with the same group of students that don't know what words like "sum," or "product" mean? Or how many major times zones there are in the U.S.? Or that France is in Europe? I've been wrong before, but I'm going to assert that you deserve better.

2) A Practical Definition of Intelligence and What They're Measuring on the Test

"[Practical intelligence is] practical in nature: that is, it's not knowledge for its own sake. It's knowledge that helps you read situations correctly and get what you want."
— Malcolm Gladwell

My father's family is from New Zealand, and when I go there it is not uncommon to see a cricket match, a very popular sport in that part of the world. Now, when I sit down with my extended family to watch a game, I gather that I'm having a very different experience than the other people there. The other people are much more mindful of what's going on in the match, be it the strategies in play or the execution of those strategies. My family is also mindful of the comments the sports commentators make and even have a second-level meta-commentary on the verisimilitude of said comments. They are mindful of the comments that friends and family are likely to make with each other after the match. They even have an intergenerational perspective of how their parents or grandparents would interpret the match. By way of contrast, if you sit me down in front of a television with them to watch a match, I will miss all of this.

Pictured: I have no idea what is happening here.

Now, some people are inclined to argue that I miss these things because I am not very bright, and they could be correct. They might, for example, point out that cricket floats between the second and the fourth most popular sport on the planet, and that I miss the "obvious" things that roughly three hundred million fans worldwide (many of whom are illiterate) find intuitive.

While all this might be true, I favor another explanation. In full disclosure, I owe a great debt to Bart A. Baggett and his excellent books for illuminating this for me. Please follow the following exercise to better understand one of the cognitive supports of this book. I promise that it will be valuable to your studies and beyond.

Please take a moment to look at the following picture before continuing, and while you're there, make a quick count of the number of circles in the picture before proceeding.

Got your answer? Great. There were six circles. Did you get it?

Now, without looking back, try to remember the amount of triangles. A little more difficult, isn't it?

Can you remember the amount of squares in the picture? The number of acute angles? I'm guessing not. (That's very impressive if you did, by the way.)

There's nothing wrong in your brain or perception. We simply all have a "gatekeeper" in our mind that sorts out what information is or is not relevant to us at any given moment. While you were focused on circles, your mind simply wasn't paying attention to the squares or the number of triangles. You were simply not mindful of the squares when you went through the exercise.

One way of thinking about my relatives' excellent level of acumen with cricket then is to posit that they have trained themselves to be mindful of the relevant details and, importantly, mindful to improve and expand upon their fluency with those details as time passes. Whenever a match is going on for them, the gatekeepers in their minds simply find the relevant data for them and spend the desired cognitive bandwidth on processing and analyzing that data. I simply have never done this as, growing up in a different country with different popular sports, there was very little in my youth to point to me that any of this was relevant to my situation.

I'm going to argue that this is really all there is to intelligence. That is, being mindful of the not-quite-arbitrary criteria that most people agree defines a cogent cognitive landscape.

By way of example, when I was young, I was taught chess, and to some people that makes me seem more intelligent. I am going to argue that a person can succeed at chess to a surprisingly high degree with memorizing what I'm going to call cut-and-paste strategies, which is simply an attentiveness to a certain set of details. Even so, for a very long time, when people found out that I played chess, they seemed to hold me in higher intellectual esteem. Memorizing a few pre-set strategies is not a huge feat of human cognition. Interestingly, now that a computer has beaten the world champion at chess, I don't know that the game has the same intellectual prestige that it used to. Before that event, we might have said that it took herculean amounts of study and focus to play at the highest levels. But I think chess's crown has been tarnished a little into "something a computer could do." My personal sense is that our definition of intelligence includes a little bit less linear focus and a little bit more creativity now.

Interestingly, a computer has now beaten the world champion in the game of "go," a much less linear and more "human" game. That speaks volumes in my mind as to how far we come with artificial intelligence, but, unfortunately, that subject is beyond the scope of this book.

I'm going to argue here that if you want to succeed at the test, you don't necessarily need to be all that "smart" as much as you just simply need to be mindful of the details that go into the test that you're studying. Fortunately for us, there are a great many excellent options and training methods available to us on how to best test. I don't know which test you're taking, but I am positive that there are books, classes, tutors, video lectures, and workbooks available to you. You are simply going to have to be mindful and cognizant of the things that they teach you.

To do this, we are going to have to examine two more issues: the reasons behind why you want to succeed and the details of your study regimen. I hope to expand upon these latter two subjects at great length in later chapters.

For the time being, I'd like to leave you with a few questions to encourage the gatekeeper in your mind to focus on the relevant details it will take to be a top achiever. I will refer to these questions as "magic questions" throughout the book.

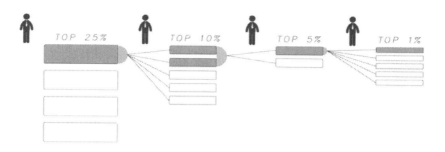

Do you have a particular category of how you'd like to score? The top 25%? 10%? 5%? 1%? Take a moment to decide which category is best for you.

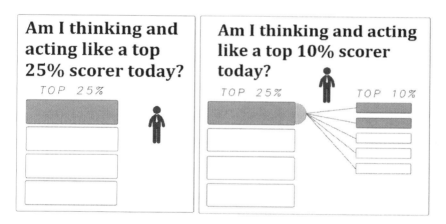

Am I thinking and acting like a top 25% scorer today? Am I thinking and acting like a top 10% scorer today?

Am I thinking and acting like a top 5% scorer today? Am I thinking and acting like a top 1% scorer today?

3) Not Getting Left Behind: The Myths and Realities of Standardized Tests

The challenge of modernity is to live without illusions and without becoming disillusioned.
— Antonio Gramsci

I am in the unfortunate position of having to explain that you've been deceived. The stylized reality that Hollywood and the entertainment industry want you to believe is that "life" happens roughly between the ages of 16 to 25.

According to them, this is where you discover yourself, make friends, fall in love, succeed or fail at sports, learn to sing, learn to dance, start your career, get engaged or married, take the vacation you will remember forever…and so on. So, a diagram of what they want you to believe might look something like this:

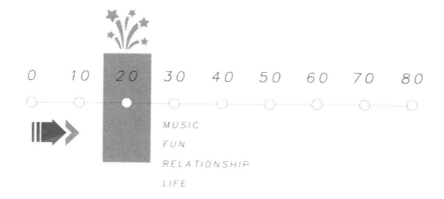

This is unfortunate because, as any mature adult can tell you, life doesn't really start until you start earning your own income, and that typically doesn't start until after you're finished with school. So, a better map might look like:

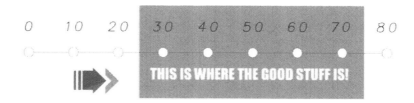

One way of thinking about this, assuming that you are in high school or college, is to think back to when you were in elementary school or junior high. Although those memories and decisions obviously shape you, you would probably agree that they are simply less relevant to your current identity and situation. You probably now have more powerful memories from more recent events to guide and shape your days.

This is important because when you take a test like the SAT, ACT, SHSAT, GMAT, GRE, LSAT, NCLEX, or MCAT, you're really investing in and shaping important events in your adult life.

Is the bulk of your life worth the investment? Is having a rich and fulfilling life worth finding the time for?

The Top 40%

According to a 2012 study performed by a job placement firm, 60% of college graduates cannot find meaningful work in their chosen field of study. In fact, a recent issue of *Consumer Reports* magazine was titled "Student Debt, Lives on Hold" quoted one alumni as saying, "I feel like I kind of ruined my life by going to college." The message is pretty straightforward: you don't want to go to college if you're not going to extract something valuable out of it.

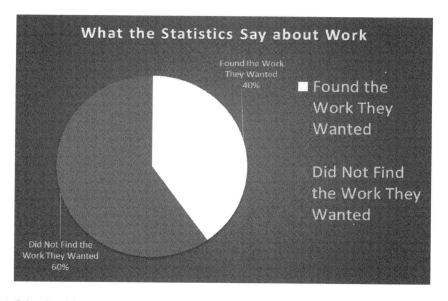

This signifies a lot of trends coming together, but this is probably not as bad as it sounds. I would argue that more than 60% of high school graduates also do not find meaningful work in their chosen field of study. One way of thinking about this is to say that the system is not fair in that it doesn't provide milk and sweet cakes for all of your work. Another way of thinking about this is that you probably want to do better than the bottom 60% in your chosen field of work.

The world is simply too competitive now for a strategy of staying in the middle. This is particularly dangerous because most students prefer to hide somewhere in the middle of their friends with regard to grades and test scores. Students don't want to have the lowest score, but they surprisingly also don't want to be the person with the highest score. This is fine if you and your friends hang out in the top 1 to 5% or so, but more dangerous if you're like most people. At the risk of sounding elitist, I'm also going to argue that you don't want to be in the bottom 75% either.

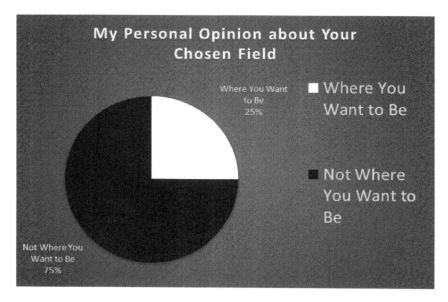

By way of comparison, you might look at a competitive chart for athletes. I'm going to argue that only the top 1% or so of high school athletes make it into college athletic tracks, and that only about 1% of those go on to play professionally. There are probably similar statistics for politics.

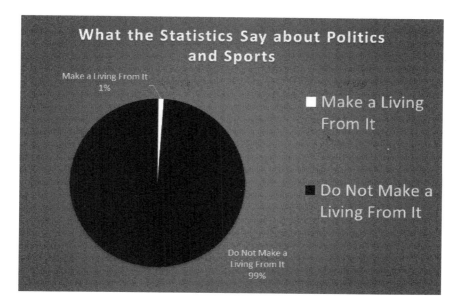

The Illusion of Safety

This issue is exacerbated by the school environment in that there's a particular deceit in the grading system. The national statistics about most schools in this country say something like this.

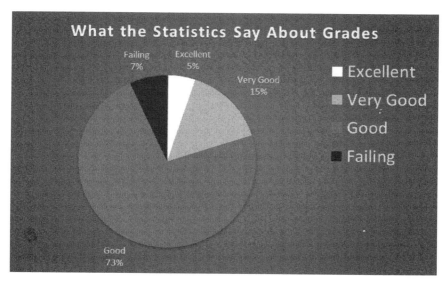

However, most students see something like the following.

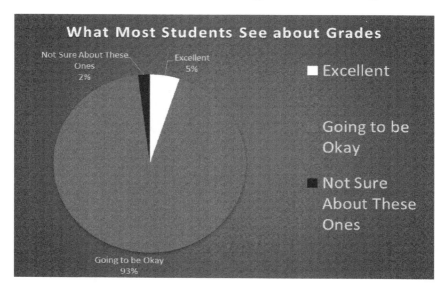

This is especially true if your school is inflating the grades of your "student athletes" to keep the federal regulators out of the picture. Simply put, it's not that difficult to graduate high school. The deceit is that having a high school diploma has almost no value on its own, and that the competitiveness of the job market almost precludes anyone in the bottom 60 to 75%.

One approach to this is to wish that the world was more fair and appreciative of your unique genius. Another approach is to raise your standards and improve your skillset.

Choosing to Take the Path

Having once been young, and meeting as many students as I do, I can say that it's very easy to look at a test or study regimen like this and see it as "one more thing that I have to do that someone else is making me do."

I would also say that, on the balance of things, this sort of study regimen is not the sort of thing that most people "want to do." I would even argue that it's a bit of a trap to pretend to "want to study" as a way of motivating yourself through this process. It might get you started, but I think that it's thin gruel to sustain you.

I'm going to argue here that there's a third path. Even if this sort of thing is not something that you would ordinarily want to do, and even if it's something that other people are making you do, I'm going to ask you to make the very powerful decision of deciding to do it. You can, under your own power, decide that you are going to do this. This is a choice. You could also choose to rebel or self-sabotage.

Interestingly, you might find that the people who are normally trying to force you to do things now slow you down. It is courteous to ask them to move before you push them aside.

Stand on your own two feet. You might like the view. :)

4) Taking your Future Seriously: The Inner Game of Beating the Test

I've missed more than 9000 shots in my career. I've lost almost 300 games. 26 times, I've been trusted to take the game winning shot and missed. I've failed over and over and over again in my life. And that is why I succeed.
— Michael Jordan

I hope to explain here why I think that the standardized tests are crucial to acquiring a rich and fulfilling life in our modern society.

While other authors might be inclined to opine here about the history of standardized tests and the virtues of the higher education, I would prefer to start somewhere else.

I can boil down the reasons to why the test should be important to you to four words.

Because you are important.

That's it. Twenty-two letters.

B-E-C-A-U-S-E Y-O-U A-R-E I-M-P-O-R-T-A-N-T.

This is your life. The SAT/ACT is one of the first steps most students take into adulthood. I'm also going to write that even if you don't reach your score, or for some reason decide not to go to college, getting through this process can be one of the most empowering experiences in your life.

The process of identifying where you are in relation to your goals (something we might call point A) and mastering new material to maneuver yourself to where you want to be (something we might call Point B) is essentially what successful adults almost exclusively spend their time doing. I challenge you to name one hero or role model who did not go through this process. What Point B becomes does change as you move through your life and become more successful, but why not start now and get good at the process while you're still young?

But before I get into how to get through this process, I'd like to write a little about why I think Point B, with regard to a high test score, is so important.

When the tests were first developed, there were a great, great many more living-wage jobs available to people who didn't go to college. There were even a great many ways to make a living that didn't involve so much as a high school education. As it so happened, one of my grandfathers led a very rich and fulfilling life without so much as completing elementary school. He lived and died a happy man surrounded by friends, a loving family, a supportive community, and a great many happy grandchildren and great-grandchildren.

Looking good, Grandpa!

Times have changed. Imagine if one of your good friends had dropped out to work at around the sixth grade. Would you predict a rich and fulfilling life for him? Would you expect the two of you to stay in the same town, keep in touch, and remain in the same group of rock-solid friends into your old age? Would you all expect to retire to the same retirement community and sip shanties into your twilight years? My guess is that you wouldn't. One of the prices we pay for our advanced society and unprecedented personal affluence is a comparatively long time spent in study and education (and a dispersed society, but that subject is beyond the scope of this book).

The fact of the matter is that, in our current society, those canals and waterways to a rich and meaningful life have more or less silted up. To gain access to the enormous wealth and rewards of our knowledge-based society, you must be able to gather, process, synthesize, and communicate the information relevant to the task at hand. Standardized tests like the SAT, ACT, SHSAT, GMAT, GRE, LSAT, NCLEX, and MCAT measure your capacity to do exactly that, and they're a mechanism to publicly showcase your intelligence. Fair or unfair, the tests have become a major key to the typical person's success.

Another component of this issue is that, in our increasingly stratified society, almost all of the income, privilege, and power go right to the top. This is not a fair, natural, inevitable, or even necessarily a stable state of affairs, but that subject is (again) beyond the scope of this book. For the purposes of our objectives, I'm simply going to assert that this is the situation we're in. My goal with this book is less to change the system than to help you advance as far as you can within that system. As someone who believes in equal opportunity for all of our citizens, please save any efforts on your part to promoting a fair and open society for when you're done with the test. We have enough work with the task at hand.

Perhaps I can offer a sports analogy. The highest paid athlete at the time of this writing is Floyd Mayweather, who made $300,000,000 in the past year as a boxer. That is almost a third of a billion dollars and more money than the cumulative net wealth acquired through a lifetime of landed privilege and political connections of either presidential candidates John Kerry ($280 million) or Mitt Romney ($220 million). The next highest earning boxer on the list I'm reading is Manny Pacquiao, with $41.8 million dollars in earnings; an enormous amount, but less than a sixth of the number one boxer and not even a fifth of the presidential nominees. The next highest ranking boxer is Wladimir Klitschko, who earned $28 million, which is not even 75% of the previous contender and less than a tenth of the first ranked. By the time you get down to Tyson Fury, the 10th ranked (in the world), he's making only $5 million a year. $5 million a year is a considerable amount of money, but let's put that in perspective. If you were to somehow take all of Tyson Fury's money at the end of a year (and good luck with that, by the way) and then somehow prevent yourself (and Tyson) from aging, send him out to fight for another year, take that money, and then repeat that process every year, you would have to do this process 599 times before you acquired all the money made by the top boxer in one year. You would still be repeating this process into the 2700s. Most science fiction does not brave to speculate that far ahead. I do not profess to be able to change the system. My goal and purpose with this book is to move you as far up the ranks as I can. We will have more opportunity to reform the system from the inside.

We are trying to shape events very far in the future with our efforts here.

Our democratic society is built upon the foundation of an informed and active citizenry. Even if it wasn't, securing and retaining a rich and fulfilling life should be your first priority. I am simply arguing that the requisite skillset to obtain a high standardized test score is a valuable tool to that larger purpose. No one is going to hand you a rich life. No one *can* hand you a rich life.

Vision and Focus win the day: Mapping Your Motivation

Most students have one or two dominant categories of motivation for wanting to succeed at the test.

MONEY

RECOGNITION

ADVENTURE

SELF-PRESERVATION

They are: **Money. Recognition. Adventure. Self-preservation.**

Money: The first major benefit of succeeding is that you get to make a lot more money in life than you otherwise might. At the time of this writing, the University of Pennsylvania has produced more billionaires (with undergraduate degrees) than any other university in the country. Harvard places in first if you count post-graduate degrees. Even if you don't aspire to become a billionaire, the lifetime income of college graduates typically far exceeds that of non-graduates.

Recognition: Another great benefit to doing well is the recognition from friends and family and the people who support you. I meet a great many families and, while all parents love their children, you can put an extra bounce in the step of your family and friends by achieving something of real substance. People like winners. Your roommate in college might even introduce you as the one who got the top score.

Adventure: Another great benefit succeeding is the chance to go on an adventure. A big advantage of conquering such a rigorous mental obstacle course is that you get to hang out with other people who made it. I'm told that education at certain schools is not very much more excellent than other places that offer excellent educations; the major difference is the type of people you can rub elbows with and the world that they inhabit. Would anybody like to spend some time as a roommate with the future Secretary of State? How about an Olympic athlete? How about having the world leader in applied robotics as one of your professors? One major issue to tackle is that when you let your hair down, who are you letting it down with?

Self-preservation: The final main category to consider deals with self-preservation. The reality of today's job market is that 60% of college graduates cannot find relevant or lucrative enough work in their chosen field of study. In my mind, this is more harsh than it seems. I say this because this is mostly true of high school educations as well. The bottom 60% of high school graduates don't typically turn out to have a rich and rewarding life either. In fact, this is fantastically less competitive than the entertainment industry, where as I understand less than 1% or make a living, and even then only for a brief period of time. Some will argue that this is symptomatic of larger troubling trends subsiding beneath the surface of our society, and they could be correct. My suggestion is to say that you don't want to be in the bottom 60% of any category that you decide is important to you. At the risk of sounding elitist, I would also argue that you ideally don't want to

28

work in the bottom 75% either.

Getting Crystal Clear about Your Motivation

We need to get crystal clear at this point as to why you're taking this initiative on. Be honest with yourself. Even if the answer is ultimately "get my parents off my case," it's your reason, and that's good enough. That said, if that's your situation, I challenge you to look for other complementary reasons such as the ones previously mentioned in the book. Most people gravitate towards one or two of the above categories: The opportunity for tremendous wealth. The fun and prestige of getting your body of work recognized. The adventure of living life to the fullest surrounded by fun and exciting people. Or, you might simply write down the simple desire to not get left behind with what could be a life of wage-slavery. Once you generally know why you want your score, I'd like to encourage you to anchor that with some specifics.

Please write down as many reasons as you can for why you want the outcome you want. I've included a brief worksheet here and again in Appendix C. Once you've written these reasons down, you then want to winnow that list to three or four. You're looking to focus only on the reasons that get you out of bed, and most of the initial reasons people come up with are not so valuable. You want as much clarity and focus as possible here. If you're in this for the recognition, think about giving speeches or having your name resonate down the ages. If you're in this for the money, can you picture upscale condos in New York City or $750+ hamburgers? Whatever it is, you want to be able to get started on your success system every day.

The "Why You Want It" worksheet

The "Why I Want It" Worksheet

Top 15) Why Do You Want This Score?	Top 8) Why Do You Want This Score?	Top 4) Why Do You Want This Score?
1	1	1
2	2	2
3	3	3
4	4	4
5	5	
6	6	
7	7	
8	8	
9		
10		
11	What are Your Highest Motivation Catgories?	
12	Money	
13	Adventure	
14	Recognition	
15	Self-preservation	

Target Score or School:

What do you expect to have to do to achieve this?

Is there anything you're going to have to give up to get there?

Do you commit to this process?   Yes/No

Visualizing Your Success Process

It's then useful to note what your target score or school is and the steps you're going to have to take to get there. What new things are you going to have to do to achieve this? Is there anything you can expect to give up as you go through this process? I will ask you to formally commit to this process later in the chapter, but it's good to know if you commit to this process now.

The Language of "I Don't Have the Time"

Some students will say to me, "I'd really like to bring home the score, but I really don't know that I have the time." Most of my students are very busy. When I hear this language, it speaks to me of not having sold yourself on your own vision or having the right reasons for why you're interested.

I don't know what your priorities are, but let me again reiterate the importance of standardized tests. You essentially have three categories of things that help you get to college: your grades or GPA, your community work, and your test scores, with your test scores typically weighing the most.

If your priorities look something like this…

1) Test score
2) GPA
3) Social life
4) Community service
5) Sports

… then you're going to have a very different situation than if your priorities look like this:

1) Chipotle
2) Baseball practice
3) Social life
4) That one very interesting person in second period Spanish class
5) School stuff

If you find yourself in this second camp, but you genuinely want to be in the first, I have a little exercise that might help you.

A Great Exercise for a Preoccupied Mind

If you find yourself with too many things on your mind, one way to effectively deal with the issue is to get it all out on paper. This will do two things. It will take the fear out of most of what is going on in your mind, and it will give you a much better path to succeeding at your goals, as you can pick them up and put them down and triage them much more effectively.

I recommend that you acquire a sheet of poster board and some multicolored sticky notes. If poster board is unavailable, a sheet of paper will do. You want to write down everything that's bothering you or is on your mind.

BRAINSTORM

You then want to triage them in some sort of rank of priority.

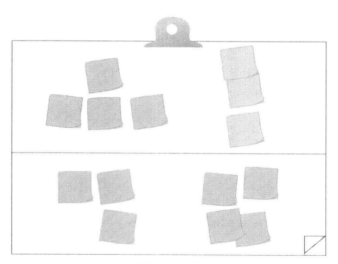

TRIAGE

Another useful technique is to put all the issues that are on your mind in one color, and then put all the action steps that go into those issues in a second color.

The 72°F Room in your Head

One great way of approaching this is to imagine that you have a 72°F room somewhere in your head and that in that 72°F room you can calmly and strategically plan out what you need to do. Then, once you have that plan formed and written down, you simply want to execute that plan. So, you want to have two "selves" with this approach, the planner and the worker. All the planner has to do is think about how to best approach the situation, and all the worker has to do is keep her head down and follow the plan.

It is very powerful to divide your cognition into these two categories. The next benefit of keeping and maintaining and working a system is that you end up creating your own situation in life rather than reacting to the one you inherit. I call this "proscripting" your life. That is, you're proactively shaping the events in your life the way you want them. I understand that this is a non-standard use of the term. I am simply trying to demarcate a way of thinking that "proactively scripts" and shapes the events of your life rather than merely describing or reacting to events. I encourage you to try it. You might find that you like it a great deal.

Can you get into that 72°F room and visualize the obstacles you expect to face? Can you think of the ways you're going to conquer those obstacles? Can you visualize yourself succeeding in your studies? Can you get into that 72°F room and decide that you're going to win?

Making the Commitment

Now that we have an idea why you want to do it, can you make commitment to do it? Obviously, you can shout out to the world and make a big proclamation to your parents and friends, but the most important commitment you can make is to yourself. Do you have a quiet voice inside you? Most people do. Have the two of you agreed that this is something you want? You probably shouldn't proceed until you can get a "yes" out of that answer. In fact, if you can't get even that small level of consensus, you might consider setting up a time to chat with your inner voice before moving on in any direction with your life. We are trying to shape events very far in the future here.

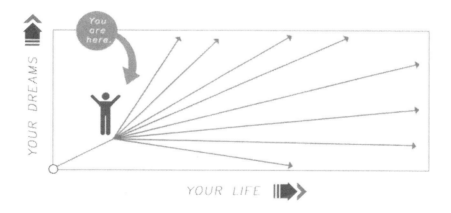

Once you've figured out why you want to do it and have made the commitment to invest in yourself, we can finally talk about how you're going to do it. Compared to figuring out why you want it, this next part is pretty straightforward. We are going to simply take a look at the score you want and the time you have and work backwards.

The path is long and narrow, and the gate is small, but I want you to know that I'm rooting for you and wishing you the best.

5) What to Expect as you March Forward: The Three Phases of Studying

The best preparation for tomorrow is to do today's work superbly well.
— William Osler

After tutoring hundreds and hundreds of students, I can confidently assert that there are three broad phases to a study regimen, and that each phase has its own rewards and pitfalls.

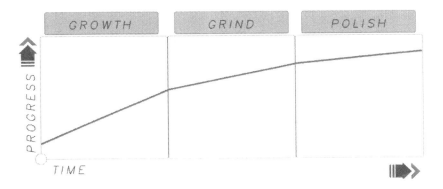

There are **The Growth, The Grind,** and **The Polish.**

Growth: The first phase is growth. Here the gains are fairly easy and straightforward. You get to see the bump in your score day-by-day and sometimes even hour-by-hour. That typically feels pretty good. If you learn a formula, chances are that you will have a chance to successfully apply it very soon.

The danger here is that you can be so confident about this process and how it's going to work for you that you don't necessarily feel any urgency to start or stay consistent. Have you ever met an athlete who was so confident about his or her chances in the fall season that he didn't bother to work out all summer? Don't let that be your story.

It is an unfortunately common trap. Many people fail to perform simply because they think they have plenty of time. Most people have procrastinated on a term paper at one point in time and come out "okay" on it. I'm going to argue that a test like this is typically more relevant than any term paper because your term paper grade is averaged into your GPA. You don't want to procrastinate when it counts, do you? If you do, it's not entirely clear to me as to why you're reading this book.

The key to managing the Growth phase is to start early and know that it's going to get more difficult as you proceed.

The Grind: The next stage is the grind. It's almost inevitable that you will come to a plateau in your studies. You study just as much as before but have trouble scoring past a certain number, or your rate of increase slows dramatically for the same amount of work. Welcome to The Grind.

This is the obstacle most students never cross. Just to recap, if you've gotten this far, you've outcompeted anyone who hasn't studied at all and you're on par with the people that have set aside some time and put some effort into the material. At this juncture, the remaining competitors are tougher, as you're in a race now with people who are actually playing to win.

The difficulty most students have here is that they get so acclimated to the quick improvement in their scores during the growth phase that when they get to their first real challenge they're not ready for it. Many of them are surprised and confused, or they rationalize and mistakenly believe that that is as good as they can do. The reality of the situation is that some concepts are going to be more difficult than others, and that once you're mastered all the easy material, there's nothing left but the harder material. The other side of that coin is that if you start mastering the more advanced material, it's inevitable that you will understand more of the test.

No one is a champion the first time they play golf. On the same token, even without any lessons, a person who went from never having played to having played ten games would likely get better just by being mindful as they went. However, if you want to compete at a high level, you will have to start all the lessons, training, lifting (yes, professional golfers lift), hire a swing instructor, get a fitness coach, nutritionist, and all the other things that competitive athletes do.

With regard to the test, you are likely to go from learning a straightforward equation that you subsequently practice once or twice a test to learning an advanced equation that you might only come across every second or third test. The key here is staying true to the commitment and plan you worked out in your planning phase. If you've segregated out the time to study, this is the time to study new and more advanced material. The best thing you can do here is stay dedicated to your study plan and make sure that you hit your numbers every week. Staying the course wins the day here.

The key to managing the Grind phase is to break it down into small daily steps and then manage those daily targets.

The Polish: The final stage of study for the test is again probably more psychological than actually cognitively difficult. Welcome to The Polish.

If you've stayed true to your plan and pushed past everything you thought you could, you probably have a much better score now and some triumphs behind you. You can start to think you're ready for a little time to celebrate. Your friends are calling. Your friends have a number of interesting and exciting ideas about what you can do with your time besides studying for the test. And they're probably right. Hanging out with them and letting your hair down probably would be more "fun" in the moment than staying on track with your study regimen. This is the pitfall of the polish phase, and it is the obstacle that will or will not set you apart from the most advanced students. Mind you, I'm not trying to imply that your friends are bad, or that they should be neglected. I'm simply saying that studying for a test is not like riding a bike, and that losing site of your targets now degrades the quality of the investment you've made in yourself. By way of contrast, if you're still hitting your targets, please make sure to go out and get some quality rest and recreation time. Please simply remember to protect your investment.

By way of example, you may remember the scandal in 2009 around Michael Phelps getting caught smoking marijuana. I want to say that he had earned about eight Olympic medals at that point in time. If I remember correctly, the reaction at the time was largely mild. He probably lost a million and a half dollars in sponsorships that year, and he probably learned a few valuable lessons about the quality of his friends and entourage (those that took the picture and sold it for a quick buck), but I don't remember any particular national outrage, and there certainly weren't any sort of criminal charges pressed against him.

I seem to remember most people at the time saying that Phelps was simply a good person with a demanding life who made a few unfortunate decisions. I do not know, but I suspect that the reality is that if you bring home eight (or more) Olympic medals there are probably a variety of things you can get away with that would get other people arrested.

That said, let's look at this from another perspective. Imagine that those pictures were taken and came out a few days before the Olympics started. How might the opinion of the man who was to represent the United States in swimming that year be different if he had been caught ditching practice to smoke weed days or hours before competition time?

The keys to managing the Polish phase are to revisit your motivation & goals often and to plan for some sort of celebration after the fact because the temptation and trap of the Polish phase are to take time off before and coast before game day. Please remember that champions celebrate *after* the win, not before.

Staying Mindful and On Task

Every one of the above phases has its own rewards and pitfalls, but the key to all of this is to stay committed to your goals. I hope to give you more tools to do so in the following chapter.

6) Your Secret Superpower: Your Success System

Success is nothing more than a few simple disciplines, practiced every day.
— Jim Rohn

We've all seen the video of the superspy dusting off some bullet wounds to take down the bad guy after he remembers some emotional moment, or the soldier who defeats impossible odds after watching his comrade die in battle. Unfortunately, this is mostly the stuff of movieland. Unless you're a fictional character, the truth about emotions and motivation is that they really don't get you very far on their own. Granted, heightened emotion and soaring motivation are great tools for clarifying what you want and what you need to do, but in real life there is almost no situation where someone achieves something difficult by being particularly emotional or motivated. In fact, quite the opposite is true, as almost all great achievements are composed of countless small decisions made toward that goal.

What you need is a system for focusing and coordinating those countless small decisions. You need a success system. Without it, the overwhelming odds are that you'll get into a cycle where your feelings at the moment control which way those decisions go, and you're left with a lack of focus and confusion. If your immediate feelings control your immediate decisions, which control your actions from hour to hour, these actions will then in turn shape your feelings, which will in turn determine your next round of

41

decisions and actions, which in turn determines your feelings ad infinitum.

You've probably seen people or animals like this in your life, and it's no way to achieve anything of any value. It's like a dog chasing his tail.

Pictured: Not what you want in life.

What you want is a clear idea of your decisions to lead the way. Add a little grit and willpower, and your decisions will then lead into actions, which will then produce the feelings.

This is a incalculably better approach to life and it will put you ahead of most people.

By way of example, the first test-prep book I ever wrote took 200 hours of face-time in front of the computer to complete. I know this because I broke my work segments into 30-minute chunks which I measured with the timer on my phone. For every 30-minute focused block of writing time, I would put a little mark down on my calendar. At the end of this process, I had 400 little marks.

2 |||| |||| I	3 |||| ||||	4 ||||	5 |||	6 ||	7 |||| I	8 |||| ||
9 |||| |||| I	10 ||	11 ||||	12 ||||	13 ||	14 ||||	15 ||||
16									17					18				19			20			21					22				

Not a bad three weeks, I thought.

In response to the people who rhapsodize about how a person needs to be passionate about their day to day life and every choice they make, I can tell you that the amount of times I felt passionate sitting down to write my book accounted for perhaps three of those four hundred tick marks. Maybe four. And yet I succeeded. I am also very "happy" with the outcome. Please notice that I didn't succeed through any superhuman feat of willpower or an amplification of my passions, but through the simple discipline of finding 30 to 90 minutes a day to sit down and write. I also receive the daily residual "happiness" of knowing I accomplished a difficult task. It is, in fact, the same system I used to write this book (and three others) in the past year. Not unlike getting to the gym, the hardest part is getting in the front door; or, with regards to the test, the hardest part is turning off your phone, sitting down at the table, and cracking open your study material. I have every confidence that you can do all three of those things. If you want to amplify this process, put a daily target on things.

From the point of view of a tutor, I will predict a win – every time – from the student who is willing to put in a daily 30 to 90 minutes over a student who blocks off all day Saturday or Sunday to study. Long blocks of study time are easy to dread, even easier to procrastinate on, difficult to pull off, and harder to remember the lessons from.

In fact, my personal opinion of what separates a good school from a bad school, be it public or private, is almost exclusively whether it has a substantive homework culture. Please understand that I don't have a "homework for homework's sake" agenda. Mindless busywork is obviously a waste of precious energy. I am simply saying that the students I meet who have a rigorous homework background already have a "success system" in place for their homework that more easily processes the study material I assign them. And, by and large, they know more of my material to begin with, acclimate to my system more quickly, complete my lessons with less effort, and get more out of it than students who come from a less rigorous environment.

With a success system, whenever you want to take on a new project, you don't have to worry about the motivation and outcome so much. All you simply have to do is get clarity on your goals, figure out when you can work towards them, and be mindful of hitting your targets and numbers on a daily, weekly, and monthly basis.

If you ask most students how much they studied last week, some of them might be able to give you an estimate, but most students simply do not know. If you then asked the typical student why they were making the sacrifice to study, they might be able to give you some vague answer as to the general importance of education, but again, you might be surprised at how vague and diffuse their answer is. This is going to be your advantage; you are going to know exactly why you're making the sacrifices, exactly how much you studied from week to week, what your current score is, and how well you're proceeding towards your target. Your system will look like a superpower to anyone who doesn't know your secret.

The Key to Conquering the Test: Preparation. Preparation. Preparation.

"You have to rely on your preparation. You've got to really be passionate and try to prepare more than anyone else, and put yourself in a position to succeed, and when the moment comes you've got to enjoy, relax, breathe, and rely on your preparation so that you can perform and not be anxious or filled with doubt."

-Steve Nash, eight-time NBA All-Star and a two-time recipient of the NBA Most Valuable Player Award

I am particularly fond of the above quote by Steve Nash because it so eloquently captures what I think are the two main components to a successful test run: focus and discipline during the preparation phase, and relaxing into your new comfort zone on game day.

I'm going to assert here that the human mind is not built to achieve long-term goals without a system or plan. One of my goals with this book is to help you create that structure. I simply want to emphasize that I think the biggest difference between a successful student and an unsuccessful one is the sort of foreground they build.

If you're going to have confidence on game day, you need to have acquired the needed level of mastery of the material and comfort inside that cognitive space. I know of no other way of getting there.

Or, in the words of Colin Powell, "There are no secrets to success. It is the result of preparation, hard work, and learning from failure."

With that in mind, let's see if we can make a system for you.

45

How Much to Study? Get to Know your "Floor Score" and Work Back

Okay, now that you know why you want to win, what is the minimum score you need to achieve that? A simple internet search of the name of the college you want, GPA, and name of the test as keywords should reveal what you need to know. Once you know that score, I suggest you aim halfway between that number and the perfect as your target. If you are already in the top 1%, then you want to aim for the perfect.

Once you have that, you simply need to get an idea of where you are now. Many students have a good idea of where they are now from previous tests and most study books have a diagnostic in the first chapter or two. It is also common to find a schedule of assignments based on how much time you have, so if that would be valuable to you, please make sure that's in the book you select.

Once you know your base score and your target score, please simply divide up the book by how long you have to study. So, if your study material has 4 lesson chapters and 6 tests and you have 8 weeks, you need to go through about 1 and a quarter sections a week to get through it all. Another approach is to simply make sure you're completing about a study book a month. I recommend that you complete all the material in at least one reputable prep book before the test. Two is better. You are investing in yourself here.

The Best Techniques to Conquer the Test

Simplify to amplify: If you're going to take your goals seriously, you want to preemptively simplify. You want a dedicated bag to carry all your study items with. You want your study books and papers together in an organized manner and without a lot of clutter.

You want an organized study regimen. You want dedicated schedule times when you know when you will be studying, and you want to know what you will be studying from day to day. (A study plan is typically easy to find at the beginning of most study books. If you're having trouble, then divide the amount of sections in the book by the amount of days you have. If that number comes to less than an hour of study material a day, you might want to add more study material.)

You want to have clear and dedicated study material. Knowing one book or workbook very well is much better than starting on two or three different books with a variety of perspectives. You want to have your study material ready to go.

You want to work in focused blocks of time, and you want to record those focus blocks of time. It feels great when you can look back at a successful study block, and you get a convenient tool to improve your study habits when you record your efforts. You want a steady, "no drama" effort. The vagaries and ravages of "extreme" motivation are needlessly difficult to manage and invite defeat. I include the worksheet that I personally use from week to week at the end of this chapter, and it includes a place at the bottom of each day to record any successes or any issues that could have been better. I will go over how to better leverage this tool in the next chapter.

You want to schedule time blocks of "fun" into your schedule and take those time blocks seriously. This will serve as a counterbalance to the dedicated study time you're carving out. I invite you to get creative here and plan something unusually fun into your week.

You want to protect your agenda. Your initiatives are important, and the reality for most people is that plenty of other day-to-day priorities are going to interfere and chip away at your time. You need to be able to say "no" at times and that you're "unavailable" at others. You don't have to be rude about this, and it's sometimes nice to give a little explanation such as "I am working on this really important project right now." You and your story are important, and you need to protect them.

You want to add the relevant "magic question" into your life. A good time to review your question is in the morning, before you go to bed, and every time you start your study material. Using index cards to remind you is an effective tool. Please find a sample one below.

You want to have a plan for "interrupting interruptions." You want to be able to detect when you're getting off course and find a path back to your high-priority work. It's a lot easier to think about this ahead of time and make the right decision than trying to do so in the moment. A simple example of this would be a situation when you typically go out for ice cream with your friends on Thursday evening after practice but know that this week you have to get some work done, and that you have trouble saying no to them. You can rehearse ahead of time in your mind how you will say "no" on Thursday or even tell everybody beforehand that you won't be able to make it that evening. This is immeasurably easier than trying to summon the willpower after practice that day

BRING HOME THE SCORE

when you want to chat with your friends and you're craving ice cream. It's very powerful to identify the things that could kill your momentum ahead of time and then take steps to avoid them.

You will need to show up and challenge yourself. One of the greatest feelings in life is challenging yourself to do something difficult and rising to your own expectations. You want to congratulate yourself for doing it, and you want to find special ways of congratulating yourself for going the extra mile.

You want to be mindful. You want to do what you can to be mindful and at ease about your situation. This particular topic is larger than the scope of this text, but I feel compelled to at least mention it here. I meet seventy-five or so families a year, and I can tell you that some of them have all of the things that most people strive for — big houses, luxury cars, expansive vacations — and yet are miserable. I also meet families who are at peace with and even invigorated by the adverse situation their particular family is in. You cannot choose the totality of your situation, but you can choose your reaction to it. This is a very valuable skill.

Next Steps

Can you visualize your plan at this point? Can you see how you're going to win this? Standardized tests have the advantage that you more or less know what the value of a high score is, but even in the situation that you can't see the value of the end result yet, I still encourage you to challenge yourself and pursue your path. Please find a template worksheet that I use to schedule and block time for my own goals below and again in Appendix C.

Our task here is not to discern what lies dimly at a distance, but to clearly focus on the task at hand

Monday	Tuesday	Wednesday	Thursday
8am	8am	8am	8am
9am	9am	9am	9am
10am	10am	10am	10am
11am	11am	11am	11am
Noon	Noon	Noon	Noon
1pm	1pm	1pm	1pm
2pm	2pm	2pm	2pm
3pm	3pm	3pm	3pm
4pm	4pm	4pm	4pm
5pm	5pm	5pm	5pm
6pm	6pm	6pm	6pm
7pm	7pm	7pm	7pm
8pm	8pm	8pm	8pm
9pm	9pm	9pm	9pm
10pm	10pm	10pm	10pm
Misc	Misc	Misc	Misc
Could Have Been Better Δ	Could Have Been Better Δ	Could Have Been Better Δ	Could Have Been Better Δ
Successes +	Successes +	Successes +	Successes +

When can I start on high-value work?

How do I want to feel when I go to bed tonight?

Friday	Saturday	Sunday	Week in Review
8am	8am	8am	Could Have Been Better Δ
9am	9am	9am	
10am	10am	10am	
11am	11am	11am	
Noon	Noon	Noon	
1pm	1pm	1pm	
2pm	2pm	2pm	
3pm	3pm	3pm	
4pm	4pm	4pm	
5pm	5pm	5pm	
6pm	6pm	6pm	
7pm	7pm	7pm	Successes +
8pm	8pm	8pm	
9pm	9pm	9pm	
10pm	10pm	10pm	
Misc	Misc	Misc	
Could Have Been Better Δ	Could Have Been Better Δ	Could Have Been Better Δ	
			Next Week +
Successes +	Successes +	Successes +	

7) The Tip of Mount Everest: Strategies for Students Already in the Top 5%

Excellence is an art won by training and habituation. We do not act rightly because we have virtue or excellence, but we rather have those because we have acted rightly. We are what we repeatedly do. Excellence, then, is not an act but a habit.

— Aristotle

Michael Phelps, winner of (at least) 22 Olympic medals for the United States, was once asked how he was able to compete at such a high level. His answer essentially was this:

"The typical training regimen for swimmers at the time essentially was to train six days a week and rest on the seventh. We figured that if I could also train on the seventh day, over the course of a year, that would be an extra 52 workouts, and over the course of four years (the time between Olympics) I would have an extra 200 or so workouts behind me and ready to push me forward."

If you're interested at being the best on your track team, then you're probably going to have to go above and beyond the training that the rest of your crew does. You might have to show up earlier, or have a better diet. Just so, the same is true in academia. If everyone else has an "A" in your class in algebra II, you're going to have to take on some more advanced topics and study directly for the test if you want to surpass them.

The Two Obstacles to the Highest Echelons

The first challenge to achieving a high score is that you are competing against more and more capable students. It's one thing to be the best swimmer at your local swimming club. It's entirely another to be the best in your district because you're now competing against all the swimmers who were the best at their local clubs. If you want to move on to state, you have to beat all of the swimmers that beat other swimmers at their local district...and so on and so on.

The other difficulty of scoring in the top tranches is that it takes more and more effort to attain a consistent level of progress. This is because you will have to master the more difficult and advanced parts of the test. A solid ten hours of study this week might only move you half or a quarter as far up the rankings as it did a month ago. Such is the price of success.

Up the River and Washing Out: Doing the "Unrequired" Work

There's no way around it, if you're going to test in the highest echelons, there's no way around doing the "unrequired work." It's the price to pay to separate you from the crowd. As our educational system gets more and more competitive, the level of mastery required to be in the top tier becomes higher and higher. By way of example, in 1989 Midori Ito, the Japanese ice skating competitor to the winter Olympics, won the event by performing a triple axel jump. You now have to perform the triple axel just to get into the competition.

One way of thinking about the issue is that getting through this process is like walking upstream in a knee-deep river.

Even as you get stronger, the current gets more and more intense the further you move upstream. All you have to do to not make it is to stop moving forward. The river will push you back.

Compete with Your Own Numbers

I once knew a diligent student who was consistently scoring in the top 3% in her practice tests.

She continued to tutor with me after her first run at the test, and when I saw her after game day I asked her how she thought the test went. She was very upset and almost tearfully told me that, "I was ready to go, but then when we started, the person next to me went through the first three pages of his section while I was still on the first! That was really intimidating!"

I was surprised when she said this because I knew this student's mental capacity and diligence with the study material very well, and the truth of the matter was that to most of the students in that room —had they been focused on her— she would have been the intimidating one. By definition, walking into the test center with a top 3% practice score, she was projected to outcompete roughly 97 out of every 100 students taking the test that day. This is not an insignificant achievement. I was especially shocked that I had to explain this to her because she was such a math wizard. I was also shocked because I had assumed that since she was already scoring in such a high range that she had put these sorts of comparisons behind her.

I think that the lesson here for us is that it's very human to compare ourselves to the achievements of others. Very human, but typically very destructive. A much more effective way of competing in this environment is to compete with yourself. If you can take the focus off of the perceived capacities of other people (we don't know the actual accuracy or final score of this other student), you can more effectively improve your score. This is a key skill for any study habits or goal you may have. Your best strategy, come what may, is to do what you can to perform your personal best. Outside of exotic events like incompetent proctors or disruptive students, your score is not dependent upon the other individuals taking the test that day.

Competing with yourself will take you much further than competing with the people in your peer group. Now, you might inspect what other people are doing in the preparation phase just to see what the norm is and where you can find an advantage, but when it's time to roll up your sleeves and get to work, you have only yourself.

In the end, my student and I got back to focusing on her own study regimen and how to put her best effort into her studies every week. Our technique was very simple. Every week, we looked to see if there was a way she could study more, or study more effectively in the same amount of time. My student ultimately took the test again, and this time she brought home a score that she was very excited about.

You want to look for ways to give yourself an advantage. I don't know your situation in specificity, but I ask you to focus your mind on things that you can do during the week that could more easily and effectively help you get to where you want to be. One of the most straightforward ways of approaching this is with a "Substitution Box."

Directly Attacking Low-Priority Behaviors: The Substitution Box

If you know that certain ingrained habits are holding you back, one powerful technique is to attack them directly with a Substitution Box.

To actively take on an undesired behavior, you want to create a diagram like the one below. Using small sticky notes and a sheet of paper can be very effective for this. You want four categories: Things I Want to Do. Things to Switch. Things I Actually Do. Things to Stop.

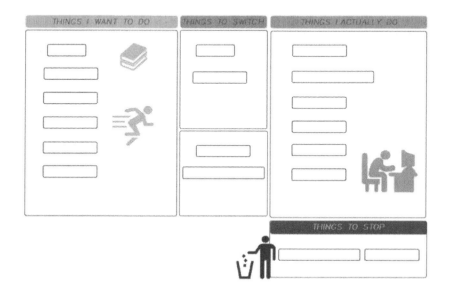

Once you have your categories, you want to fill them in with relevant topics. For example, if you know you waste too much time with mindless television, you might want to switch that habit with studying or reading. When you find yourself on the path to turning the TV on, you simply make the effort to switch tracks. If you find that the habit is too difficult to stop entirely, you might simply start trading time with it. If you know you would normally spend an hour watching television, you might let yourself watch a half an hour only after you've spent 30 minutes reading or studying.

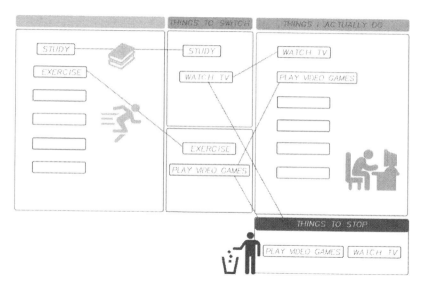

Over a period of time, the same triggers that once manifested low-value or unwanted behaviors will propel you into high-value or desired behaviors. You want to "water the flowers, not the weeds," as Sir Francis Bacon would say.

The technique is powerful because it identifies the problem behaviors and gives you a visual medium by which to manage them. The trick, though, is to limit what you're changing to one or two at a time. Overloading the process invites internal conflict and could degrade the effort.

A Morning Success Ritual

If you're really looking to add rocket fuel to your success system, I want to recommend an approach that I came across in Hal Elrod's excellent book *The Miracle Morning*. Although I hope to have given you enough tools to make a cogent method of moving forward, I'd like to share my own thoughts here on the excellent techniques in reference to creating a morning success ritual. I have seen this system work magic in other people, and I credit it with a great deal of my own personal success. I then hope to share with you some very effective techniques for the people who are not "morning persons."

Most of my recommendations, however, involve the use of a smartphone and Wi-Fi. If these two things are inconvenient for you, I encourage you to glean what you can from this template and research further techniques to develop your own process.

I'm sure that there are some readers out there who would prefer to modify this and make it some sort of after-school or after-work ritual. There are no rules here, but my experience is that it's easier for other people and priorities to chip away at your progress during those time periods. If nothing else, I encourage you to experiment with the morning ritual until such time as you can create a more excellent daily progress habit. The important thing is to build the system as soon as possible.

From a bird's eye point of view, a morning success ritual has two main values: it secures a steady stream of high-value work on your high-value priorities from day to day and week to week, and it also gives you the opportunity – as you start thinking more clearly earlier and earlier in the day – to better shape your days, weeks, and months more to your liking.

It's also reasonable to argue that if you're not willing to wake up early and work on your goals, then you probably haven't sold yourself on said goals. Perhaps your dreams are not big enough or compelling enough. I do not know your situation, but I encourage you to explore it.

An oversimplified account of the *Miracle Morning* is to say that, after some adversity, Hal Elrod looked up the most common morning habits of highly successful people and then synthesized the six most effective ones into a single morning routine. He has different names for the habits, but in abstract terms they are:

Exercise
Reading
Journaling or Writing
Affirmations
Visualization
Meditation, Prayer, or Silence

Hal simply (but powerfully) created a system to where a person could quickly and effectively perform every one of them every morning.

Exercise: I put exercise here first because it often is the foundation on which everything else is built. I recommend a warm-up with some sort of headphone-friendly exercise and combining it with listening to affirmations or audiobooks. There are also a number of excellent apps that can help you structure and track your routine. Two that I like are *Just Six Weeks* and *Sworkit*, and most modern smartphones will track your steps. A thorough workout can be the foundation of your better future. In fact, I would recommend that you have a quick and short workout before the test on game day to get the blood flowing and wake you up. I personally go through a few sets with a weighted jump rope when I need to get into the zone.

Reading: One of the most important things that separates us as humans from other animals is our capacity to focus intently on an issue. Unlike, say, dogs or camels, we can communicate about the past, the future, or even hypothetical or fictional concepts like J.R.R. Tolkien's dragons, or the statistical chances of winning the lottery. This sort of focus is exactly how we both built the Eiffel Tower and detect gravity waves in space. The advantage of reading is that you get the best of the author's thinking and that thinking can guide you to challenge and expand your own mental capacity. An easy way to work this into your daily routine is to download audiobooks to your smartphone. The public library system in my county has a free app that gives patrons the means to borrow thousands of titles from their catalogue, and my guess is that your county provides a similar service. I also subscribe to audible.com, a service that provides thousands of titles for a monthly subscription fee. For students with assigned fiction reading such as *The Great Gatsby* or *The Old Man and the Sea*, one helpful technique is to get the physical book in front of you and then listen to the audio version at about double speed as you follow along in the book. This is an excellent way to get through a book quickly and with great retention. Please also find a list of books that I think could be valuable to you in Appendix A.

Journaling: Journaling is an excellent way of staying close to your high-priority goals. It's also an excellent way of maintaining inner peace in that you get to write down and process what's on your mind. Another way to be very effective about your morning ritual is to work some sort of accountability sheet into your journaling process. I personally use a paper journal for this, but for the people who would prefer to keep digital records, the *Day One Journal* is a great app. One useful technique that I've found is to write out your three most important goals for that day and then put a special emphasis on the one thing that's most important to do that day. Some people find that this reduces their journal to a to-do list. Please find your own way. There are no rules here.

Affirmations: Some people shy away from affirmations because they seem to be something that shouldn't work. I will attest that they have worked surprisingly well for me, and that there is a great deal of excellent literature about the subject. My only innovation over what you might read elsewhere about the subject is that I've found you can record the affirmations into your phone and then have them play back to you as you are exercising or doing other work. I would recommend it to anyone who struggles with written affirmations. For readers who would want to explore this topic further, an excellent book is Shad Helmstetter's bestselling classic *What to Say When You Talk to Yourself.*

Visualization: Visualization is an interesting topic to me because the word seems to mean different things to different people. If you're in the goal-focused situation of trying to achieve a high score, an easy technique is to put a timer of 5 minutes or so on your phone and then visualize all of the good feelings around that success. Another technique is to create a "vision board" of the things that you want in your life from pictures from magazines and then quietly go over that vision board at that time. Many people have successes with either approach. The former solution takes less setup and is more portable, but some people find it worth the effort to create a physical visual board.

Meditation: The benefits of meditation are legion, and there are a variety of free or cheap apps and courses available on your smartphone or the internet. I personally like one called Meditation Studio for the iPhone, as it has a variety of quality guided meditations on a variety of topics. My recommendation would be to find one that is 15 minutes in length or less if you plan to use it daily.

I hope that I've been able to give you the resources to amplify and accelerate your capacity to reach your goals. I personally credit this process with numerous successes in my life.

For Readers Who Aren't "Morning People"

If you find yourself in the unenviable position of wanting to achieve your goals but not being a morning person, I have a number of powerful techniques to recommend. I've seen these used to great success.

The first thing I would do is to set up some sort of timer as to when you will go to bed. Yes, you want to set a bedtime.

The next thing I would do is set your alarm clock across the room.

The next thing I would do is set up a second alarm to go off after the first. Your goal is to get up between the alarms. There are many ways to customize the alarms system, both on your phone and in the wide world of consumer electronics. I personally use an alarm that starts off with a dim light and gradually increases its brightness like a sunrise in your room. I also use my phone.

If you drink coffee, plenty of coffee machines can be programmed to start as you're waking up. This can be particularly useful if you need caffeine to get out of bed.

Finally, you want to lay out your exercise clothes and a bottle or glass of water for the morning.

So, when your alarm goes off in the morning, you want to get up, walk across the room to turn it off, brush your teeth, drink your water or coffee, change into your exercise clothes, and start on your morning routine. The act of brushing your teeth and drinking your beverage typically helps a great deal with waking up.

I am also personally fond of the smartphone app Kiwake. It forces you to take a close up picture of something across the room, check your daily motivation statements, and then play a quick brain game to wake up. I have found it to be one of the most effective ways to stay on track.

A Special Technique for Recalcitrant Snoozers: Practice Makes Perfect

If you find yourself really struggling to get out of bed, it's a good idea to practice your morning success ritual. As silly as it sounds, one great way to make sure you get through your routine is to practice it during waking hours. Physically go through the process of getting up when your alarm goes off, walking across the room, brushing your teeth, drinking your water or coffee, changing into your exercise clothes, and starting on the rest of your morning routine.

Performing this while you're awake and alert is a surprisingly effective way of acclimating your mind to what you want to do automatically in the morning.

A Funny Practical Joke

One of my students was both very dedicated to studying and his life goals but also had a mischievous side to him. He was very close to his family, but he was also known as the one who liked to procrastinate on things and sleep in. Ordinarily, his mother was the first one up in the morning. He and I happened to be tutoring over his school's spring break, and as part of his new study habits and as a bit of a joke, he made sure to get up especially early and beat his mother to the breakfast table. When she came in in her pajamas or robe, he would be there fully dressed and always greet her with a chipper, "Hi Mom, I've already studied a section in my SAT book. Do you want any help with breakfast?" Or, "Hi

Mom, I went for a jog this morning and I was about to start studying but decided to set the table. Should we have pancakes this morning?" He told me that the look on her face that week was something he will never forget, and it helped set the habits and tone that he claims carried him to the Ivy Leagues (with his parents' full support, I might add). I would advise anyone who lives with his or her parents to try this for a week if for no other reason than to see the reaction.

8) Accountability: The Mother of All Achievement

Nothing in this world can take the place of persistence. Talent will not:
nothing is more common than unsuccessful men with talent. Genius will not;
unrewarded genius is almost a proverb. Education will not: the world is full of
educated derelicts. Persistence and determination alone are omnipotent.
—Calvin Coolidge

Tim Grover. Bob Bowman. Hank Haney. You may not know these names, but my guess is that you know the names of the people they shepherded into greatness, namely Michael Jordan, Michael Phelps, and Tiger Woods, respectively. I bring this up because there are persistent and pernicious myths that people make their way into excellence and the top of their profession alone. If Michael Jordan, Michael Phelps, and Tiger Woods all needed people in their support network to succeed, it's probably a good idea that you also find some support.

Even without personal trainers or coaches, one simple thing you can do to secure the results you want is to find an accountability partner. Have you ever not wanted to go to the gym or complete a group project but did it anyway because you didn't want to let your partner or partners down? However uncomfortable this can be, it's an excellent way to get you closer to your goals. I strongly recommend that you find one from your family or friends. Importantly, being at the same academic level isn't the most relevant thing here. In fact, a three-legged dog can hypothetically be more valuable and supportive during an intensive time of work then a careless "friend." That said, the dog is probably going to let you off pretty easily if you don't keep your appointment, so it's probably better to stick with friends and family.

At the risk of sounding difficult, it might also be valuable to take a clear look at your friends to see which of them generally are or are not supportive. By way of example, my cat is particularly supportive of my study/work schedule, and I am still trying to explain the square root of two to him.

No Tommy, you're still thinking in terms of rational numbers. It's irrational! The number is irrational!

Is there a study buddy that you know is dependable? Is there someone you know who is already studying for the test you're taking? The most important component is that you hold each other accountable at some level. Make sure to choose carefully; just like a workout buddy, if one person starts flagging or failing, it has a carryover effect to the other person. You also don't want to be the person to degrade someone else's trajectory. You are trying to leverage your friendships, not to bring someone down.

There are also a number of accountability apps for your smartphone. Two that I like are:

Simple Habits: This is a simple to-do list of things you want to get done or improve on every day. It has certain features like streak-counting, which are pretty good.

Productivity Wizard: This app is much more in-depth about setting up projects and getting through them.

Another powerful method of staying accountable is to create an accountability sheet of the things you want to get done in your day. It helps if you can hang it in a prominent place. Alternatively, it is also very powerful to go over your intentions for the day with your morning routine, like with your affirmations or journaling component.

The purpose of most of these tools is not so much to guide you when you're motivated – it's easy to get things done when times are great and you're motivated – as much as it is to help you stay on track when you're falling off course.

A final point that should be pretty obvious is to turn your cell phone off or put it in airplane mode during your study time. You don't want distractions creeping into this high-value time. Remember, airplane mode is not just for airplanes! :)

9) The Reach School Challenge

Every great dream begins with a dreamer. Always remember, you have within you the strength, the patience, and the passion to reach for the stars to change the world.
— Harriet Tubman

We cannot wait for the universe to move our way and allow us to succeed. We must transform the world that we've inherited into a world that we have created.

I challenge you to decide that this section of your life is going to be the one you look back on as the one when you got serious and took yourself where you wanted to go. I challenge you to decide that this part of your life is the one when you demonstrated to yourself that you could achieve these important goals. Can you decide that you're going to learn from this experience and apply it to the other challenges in your life?

Please find the worksheet that I use with my students to clarify this issue below and again in Appendix C.

The Reach School Challenge Worksheet					
School Name	Target School or Score			Current Score	

What do you want to study there?

Why do you want to achieve these goals?		What sort of fun can you work into this process?
Money Adventure Recognition Self-Preservation		
What do you expect to have to do to achieve this?		How will you reward yourself?

Is there anything you're going to have to give up to get there?

Do you commit to this process?

Remember that we're talking about an investment in yourself. This window of opportunity will not always be open for you.

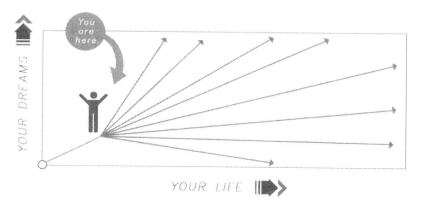

Is there anything you can do to get moving today?

69

10) Today Matters!

Success isn't a result of spontaneous combustion. You must set yourself on fire.
– Arnold H. Glasow

I want to thank you for taking the time to trust me as a resource for this process and I want to ask you to invest in yourself. If you've made it this far into the book, you're obviously interested in succeeding, and I want to congratulate you for that. I also want to ask you if there's anything further you can do *today* to reach your goals. The enemy of great is not adversity, but a comfortable situation. I'm sure you've met people who didn't measure up on game day from a simple lack of discipline, even though they had all the talent and time that they needed.

Is there anything you can do today to move you towards your goals?

Can you:

Decide on your target school or score?

Decide on the study material that you're going to use?

Prepare a dedicated study bag?

Plan your study regimen?

Schedule something fun to either do in parallel or after you've succeeded?

Develop a plan for identifying and interrupting the low-value interruptions in your life?

Add the relevant "magic question" into your life?

Make the effort to get a good night's sleep tonight?

Make the decision to invest in yourself?

If you're not ready, just do what people do after they read a book like this, and that is nothing. It's quite easy. Simple lift your feet and let the river watch you and all the work you've done downstream.

All you have to do is stop moving and let it happen.

But you're better than that, aren't you? I think you are.

Tomorrow comes today.

A Final Word of Encouragement

Not long ago in this country, the rewards of higher education were reserved for one half of the moneyed classes. Can you imagine graduating in the top 5% of your high school and having your university pass you over for a young man who doesn't know the Pythagorean Theorem? That was the power of wealth and privilege at the time. Fortunately for us, standardized testing has blunted such means of class stasis and our country now draws from an unprecedentedly large talent pool. Almost any capable and industrious student now has a chance to compete for the rewards of our larger society. I wrote these products because when my students succeed, I get to feel like I've been a part of a larger success story. Please know that I'm rooting for you. I hope my little book helps you along your way.

Appendix A: Books Towards a "Real" Education

Books I Wish Had Come Earlier to Me in My Life

If you're reading this, you're probably perceptive enough to know that most of the important things in life are not found in classrooms. You will probably have to scour the landscape for your own treasures, but I've done what I can here to identify some of the jewels I've found. I wish that I had come across these books earlier in my life.

Lessons of History by Will Durant and Ariel Durant – I can spare you a degree in philosophy, anthropology, or sociology, for you can know more in a few weeks with the wealth in Durant's work in this and other titles. This condensed piece is both accessible and compelling. Enjoy it on its own, or consider it a primer to deeper writings. Durant's works are also available on audiobook form if you prefer that medium. Another excellent text by these authors is *The Story of Philosophy*.

Choices by Shad Helmstetter – We all have habits. If you can identify the habits that are holding you back, and supplant them with ones that move you forward, you cannot help but get to where you want to go. An excellent book.

The Origins of Virtue by Matt Ridley – Matt Ridley is the former editor for the science section of *The Economist*, and words fail me in describing what an excellent book this is. In this little masterwork, Matt Ridley inverts the universe and illuminates how we, in time, interact with our very own genetic code.

The Now Habit by Dr. Niel Fiore – Another book about managing your habits. By definition, if you can direct your habits, you will have an enormous advantage over anyone that doesn't.

How to Win Friends and Influence People by Dale Carnegie – I have probably extracted more value out of this book than I can calculate. But please, do not take my word for it; see what you think of it yourself.

Rich Dad Poor Dad by Robert Kiyosaki – Another international bestseller, this book gives a unique and often unheard of perspective on money and investing. This book personally started me onto the path to financial independence. All the self-made wealthy men and women I've ever met since then have used some variation of the formula outlined in this work.

The Miracle Morning by Hal Elrod – I owe Hal Elrod a debt of gratitude in that his book outlined a great many processes that have accelerated my success, as well as the successes of many others. I would recommend it to anyone.

Best of fortunes to you, -W. Walter Tinsley

Appendix B: A Totally Serious Way to Get Free Ice Cream from the Test

Years ago I had a bright and particularly active student-athlete who (naturally) rebelled against all the time and effort she had to put into improving her score. Why can't the test just be easier?

My response was essentially as follows: What if the test didn't ask you all these academic questions, but instead scored you on how much ice cream you could eat? My student initially responded that this would be a tremendous improvement over the current state of affairs, and that more people should take these ideas seriously. I then asked her, what sort of people would get the top scores, and who would get into the top colleges?

The admissions chair at certain Ivy League schools?

Once at the top colleges, how would these students perform in that environment?

Do you really want to go to a college where the students are primarily chosen for how much ice cream they can eat? After you graduate and start looking for a job, do you really want your potential employer to see that that's the college you chose?

To finish the story, the student involved decided to study very hard, and in the end she got fully funded at an exclusive college, and she is now excelling in her line of work.

That said, if you still insist on trying to get free ice cream, my students and I have come up with the following strategy.

The Free Ice Cream Strategy

One method of approaching the test is as follows: Let's say that you are having difficulty with a particular question. Quietly pick up your test booklet and answer sheet, walk slowly over to the proctor, ask him a question about the problem you were working on, and then, regardless of his answer, kick him in the groin and demand free ice cream. This might seem nonsensical at first but, let's be honest, most people don't study very hard. The overwhelming chances are that someone else in the room is frustrated with the test and maybe even that same question. He or she might also want to get up, kick the proctor in the groin, and demand free ice cream. Nothing begets imitative behavior like a crowd; if you can get a third person up there with you it's almost guaranteed that most of the class will soon get up and surround the proctor, kicking him and clamoring for the delicious, delicious ambrosia that is free ice cream. But this is only the beginning. Think about your situation. Is it really practical to think that the proctor has enough resources or connections to acquire enough ice cream to satisfy the appetites of the crowd? Surely not. You've got to aim higher. You've also now got an excited and angry mob that feeds on free ice cream. They NEED free ice cream. How long can your position last without that fuel? The mob needs a leader. The mob needs vision.

The first thing you need to do is go outside and get the crowd to flip over a car. That shows everyone that you're serious, and it's surprisingly easy to do even if you still only have ten or so people rallied to your cause. The more cars you initially get your followers to flip, the more seriously onlookers will take you. Everyone wants free ice cream, but you're doing something about it. Gestures like these winnow out the casual and the curious and attract the true believers like ants to…well, you know. The parking lot is also advantageous in that the students taking the test in classrooms with windows facing you will be drawn to the commotion. Keep the mob shouting "FREE ICE CREAM," and with every flipped car, the spectacle of property destruction will only attract more eyes and ears to your cause. The world is almost entirely populated by people who deep-down want nothing more than to flip over cars and get free ice cream. Can you show them the way?

If the police have not already arrived on the scene, they are more or less guaranteed to be en route. This will be the most tenuous part of your journey and perhaps your moment of truth, but no one builds statues of the fainthearted in their hometown. Should you decide that you really are a man (or woman) of principles, your goal at this point is to avoid any direct confrontation with any law enforcement official, as the police have a plethora of effective ways to disperse a unified crowd. Stay in the background during this formative phase and keep things loose and decentralized for the time being. Your goal at this juncture is to grow the mob as quickly as possible so that it dwarfs the available resources of your local law enforcement. The message you need to get to the crowd and your social media platform is that "THE COPS HAVE BANNED EATING ICE CREAM AND ARE ARRESTING THE PROTESTORS!"

There is no backing down at this point. The only endgame is to march on Washington. Every time you flip over another car and demand free ice cream it will entice fresh recruits to your cause. In our hyper-connected society, once the message is out that you're marching on Washington because the government won't let you eat ice cream, it will eclipse all other "news." If you can get a video of the police arresting a photogenic young girl online, title it, "LOOK AT HOW THIS COP STOPS A GIRL FROM JUST TRYING TO EAT ICE CREAM!!!" The heat generated from the social media component of the internet will set actual fires around the country and imitators across the globe. The mainstream media are in no way too proud, moneyed, or responsible to not turn every asset at their disposal on this. Every person seeing or reading that there's a violent crowd of car-flippers marching on Washington is going to revert down to those two basic forward-thinking emotions: fear and hope. They are going to ask themselves one question: Do they want to flee the mob and its consequences, or do they want some of the delicious, delicious, free ice cream everyone else is getting? Some people will take a little time to decide, most will know pretty quickly. If you've gotten this far, you've more or less succeeded. The international media will have picked up the story and made it an international incident. This is important because it will restrict law enforcement and the military to non-lethal countermeasures. How would it look to our allies (and enemies) on the international stage if the largest and most powerful democracy on the planet fired into a crowd that only wanted a little ice cream? I challenge you to name any democratically elected government that could survive the fallout. If you're still nervous about this or you've got some sort of "law and order" firebrand in the presidency, raid some pet stores and have everyone at the forefront of the crowd hold a puppy.

Pictured: Bulletproof.

At this point, every police officer or national guardsman currently being mobilized is asking themselves one question: "Do I want to sacrifice myself to the Pyrrhic task of trying to hold back the tide of a million-strong movement of belligerent civilians with non-lethal countermeasures, or DO I WANT FREE ICE CREAM AND A PUPPY?"

It's really not that hard a decision.

You might be surprised at how many of the good men and women in our law enforcement and military dream of nothing but confronting the powers that be and getting free ice cream and a puppy out of the deal. Tacit approval of your cause, if not wholesale defections from the police and armed services, is probable if not certain.

Witness the labradoodle. Check and mate Mister President.

You now have your own security detail, police force, and military for when you're ready to sit down at the negotiating table. But what will your demands be? When they offer you ice cream at the negotiating table, turn it down, just to throw them off-guard. Just don't forget the people that got you there and all the puppies!

How do you expect to feed all those puppies? YOU CAN'T FEED PUPPIES ICE CREAM!!!

Congratulations, you have shaped the politics of this country for a generation.*

Advantages to this approach:
- You will in all likelihood get some ice cream out of it.

Disadvantages to this approach:
- Possible charges of sedition.
- Real potential for life-incarceration.
- I can't see how it's likely to improve your test score.

*(Do not do this. Do not ever resort to violence or extralegal methods to advance your test score, get free ice cream, or any other agenda you might be inclined to pursue. If you do resort to any criminal or maleficent behavior, in this or any other situation, you are on your own, legally, politically, and probably socially. Do not say that you got the idea from me. Do not imply that you got the idea

from me. Upon arrest or incarceration, do not mention me, my publisher, or anyone associated with me (or anyone) at all. You are on your own. Never turn off your critical thinking facilities in the midst of political agitators, and be especially vigilant against any political rhetoric espoused by or originating from anyone younger than thirty or any political agitator of any age who offers free ice cream. Do not involve yourself in revolutionary politics, as agents of the state will hunt you down, prosecute you in a fair or sham trial, or simply assassinate you. If I ever hear or read of your misadventures, I will laugh at how foolish and gullible you were. I will then get ice cream.)

Be careful out there. Society is surprisingly fragile. :)

Appendix C: A List of Worksheets Used

The "Why You're In It" worksheet

The "Why I Want It" Worksheet

Top 15) Why Do You Want This Score?	Top 8) Why Do You Want This Score?	Top 4) Why Do You Want This Score?
1 _____	1 _____	1 _____
2 _____	2 _____	2 _____
3 _____	3 _____	3 _____
4 _____	4 _____	4 _____
5 _____	5 _____	
6 _____	6 _____	
7 _____	7 _____	
8 _____	8 _____	
9 _____		
10 _____		
11 _____	What are Your Highest Motivation Catgories?	
12 _____	Money	
13 _____	Adventure	
14 _____	Recognition	
15 _____	Self-preservation	

Target Score or School:

What do you expect to have to do to achieve this?

Is there anything you're going to have to give up to get there?

Do you commit to this process?   Yes/No

The "Weekly Tracking" worksheet

Our task here is not to discern what lies dimly at a distance, but to clearly focus on the task at hand.

Monday	Tuesday	Wednesday	Thursday
8am	8am	8am	8am
9am	9am	9am	9am
10am	10am	10am	10am
11am	11am	11am	11am
Noon	Noon	Noon	Noon
1pm	1pm	1pm	1pm
2pm	2pm	2pm	2pm
3pm	3pm	3pm	3pm
4pm	4pm	4pm	4pm
5pm	5pm	5pm	5pm
6pm	6pm	6pm	6pm
7pm	7pm	7pm	7pm
8pm	8pm	8pm	8pm
9pm	9pm	9pm	9pm
10pm	10pm	10pm	10pm
Misc	Misc	Misc	Misc
Could Have Been Better Δ	Could Have Been Better Δ	Could Have Been Better Δ	Could Have Been Better Δ
Successes +	Successes +	Successes +	Successes +

When can I start on high-value work?

How do I want to feel when I go to bed tonight?

Friday	Saturday	Sunday	Week in Review
8am	8am	8am	Could Have Been Better Δ
9am	9am	9am	
10am	10am	10am	
11am	11am	11am	
Noon	Noon	Noon	
1pm	1pm	1pm	
2pm	2pm	2pm	
3pm	3pm	3pm	
4pm	4pm	4pm	
5pm	5pm	5pm	
6pm	6pm	6pm	
7pm	7pm	7pm	Successes +
8pm	8pm	8pm	
9pm	9pm	9pm	
10pm	10pm	10pm	
Misc	Misc	Misc	
Could Have Been Better Δ	Could Have Been Better Δ	Could Have Been Better Δ	
			Next Week +
Successes +	Successes +	Successes +	

The "Reach School" worksheet

The Reach School Challenge Worksheet				Current Score	
School Name	Target School or Score				

What do you want to study there?

Why do you want to achieve these goals?

Money
Adventure
Recognition
Self-Preservation

What sort of fun can you work into this process?

What do you expect to have to do to achieve this?

How will you reward yourself?

Is there anything you're going to have to give up to get there?

Do you commit to this process?

ABOUT THE AUTHOR

W. Walter Tinsley got his start in tutoring volunteering at an inner-city alternative school for troubled youth in the ethnic ghettos of south Dallas. There he met twelve-year-old felons, pregnant and tattooed thirteen-year-olds, bare knuckled race-posturing, and more child neglect and abuse than is comfortable to remember. (As a quick word of advice, if you ever need to contact Child Protective Services, please simply fax a report in. It's easier for them to triage written reports, and you'll save yourself about ninety minutes of hold time. As a general rule, they're much too busy, understaffed, and underfunded to take your phone call.)

It was an eventful year. Once, a particularly disinhibited student found himself at school unusually early and, finding our room empty, he retrieved the brown paper towels from the bathroom, put them in a trashcan, set them on fire, and then pushed the trashcan next to the bookcases to set as much of the school ablaze as possible. Fortunately, he was not a particularly competent fire-maker and we were able to avert the crisis when we arrived.

Still, somewhere in the confused, harassed, ghettoized, and neglected people, I still found what I think is the human spirit: one that could laugh, one that could listen quietly, one that could build, rebuild, and rebuild again. If you're out there, I wrote this little book for you.

Made in the USA
Middletown, DE
26 May 2017